THE UNRAVELING OF AMERICA

poems

Paul Christensen

Cyberwit.net
HIG 45 Kaushambi Kunj, Kalindipuram
Allahabad - 211011 (U.P.) India
http://www.cyberwit.net
Tel: +(91) 9415091004
E-mail: info@cyberwit.net

Printed at Vecore.

Dedicated to my children Maxine, Signe and Cedric, in the hopes they may live to see a sea change in American life

CONTENTS

ONE

**I tuck a pillow of dirt under your
head, a shard of jade for your slender neck.**

PLANTING TIME

Lie down in my bed, dear seedling.
You are tired from all the crying
in the nursery. You need to rest
awhile, to let your stem stretch out
to a friendly god. Your nodes
hunger to wave their arms and feel
the air, the tiny tongues
of rain, each glittering particle
dawn adorns you with. But first,
I tuck a pillow of dirt under your
head, a shard of jade for your slender neck.
Your mind is heavy with dreams
soon to be traced under your green hood.

Stars spin thin luminous threads
across the emptiness. The wind composes
humming incantations over death.
The rivers stop to listen to the hush
of the water's breath, as something
rises from the void of time.
Soon, the mountains shiver
as spring passes its velvet glove.
An ovation of wings brings up the sun
as you slowly come to know yourself.

FIVE O' CLOCK BLUES

The clouds are as wrinkled as an old man's neck.
The sun rises wearily each morning
over the abandoned fields. A deer hesitates
to walk on the road, but puts down
one slender foot and dares the hunters
to shoot her. Her fear is wasted.
No one is looking out the window.
The guns are rusting in a cabinet.

A daughter preens in the mirror,
but doesn't believe what she sees.
She's tired of being young. So is her brother.
They sit in silence waiting for a call.
The city is decaying, an old ferry
lugging its cargo of passengers
to an empty shore. Is there anyone
out there who can save us?

I used to talk to strangers but they
resented being torn from loneliness.
Don't let your eyes wander into someone new.
You may not want to know what lies behind
the question of your interest.
Best to step out of line at the market
without saying why. Let the woman behind you
go ahead, and in our silence, we owe nothing.

Home is the haven of shadows, each growing
longer in the kitchen where the stove

is cold, the refrigerator empty. I hear
a knock on the door and hide behind a wall.
It might be the murderer I read about,
eager to sink his knife in me.
Lonely people lose their trust in love.
We'd rather touch the bottom of emptiness.

A PAEAN TO SPRING

Tomorrow the air will be a breath
from the mountain tops; animals
will creep from dreams
and shake off their inertia.

Nature hangs out old winter clothes
to dry, to be washed by a rain
due on Tuesday. I'm walking
an empty road to nowhere,
hoping the first tinsel streams of
spring will oil the knees of
muck-dwellers, bug hunters,
diners on algae and sedge slime,
the horned sentries hidden in the shade
of a haha below the well.

Picture the lake shivering its skin
as the sun pulls its Jacob's ladder
into the higher branches.
The living rejoice in the power
to change, to grow, commit errors
in the overture of the season;
pity the dead in moldy holes, unable
to move a finger in eternity.

ON THE WAY HOME

No one invented the airplane
in these drab apartments.
The steam engine waited
for some other place to be conceived.
Beauty had no amateur hand
tracing the slender arms
of La Gioconda or its sensuous eyes.
Just side streets and overdue bills,
a car with parking tickets
fading on a windshield. A grocery
cart stands abandoned in a vacant lot.

It's what the first indicted president
gazes on as his motorcade crawls
through traffic on the way
to the airport. A jet emblazoned
with gold letters waits for him
to climb the back stairs to return
to Florida, a wounded man, struck
by a blow to the unguarded skin
of his delusions. He sits on his leather
throne like a deposed king, while
the ordinary world bends under
the weight of drudgery, laughing
through a mask of pretended awe.

RAILROAD TRACKS AT NIGHT

Tramps used to bammer down
in an old house nearby.
The shacks muffle the talk
under a dim light. A cat slips
under a porch at the sound of footsteps.
It's east Texas condensing over
a blue flame, where water simmers.
A child cries, and someone's slippers
hiss over the cracked linoleum.

If there was a dog, it would be barking,
but the silence stands in a drain
full of stagnant moonlight.
Night is as fragile as an old woman's
breath before she drifts to sleep.
The tracks gleam on the black skin
of earth bright as a silver bracelet,
snowy as a girl's dress as she gazes
at the endless stars at night.

RUNAWAY HOUSEWIFE

A woman hitchhiking on a lonely road
clutches her coat, holding back
whatever is alluring from passing eyes.
She fears the future, but it's nothing
like the present she's escaping from.

A house of terror looms
with dark windows, a door
ajar, the kitchen without the smell
of food in its sterile air.
Nothing matters now, she thinks.

When a pickup slows and the shotgun
door cracks open, she approaches warily.
There's a kid at the wheel, wooden blocks
tied to accelerator and brake.
He has a bright, innocent face.

He asks her where she's headed,
and she whispers that it doesn't matter.
They drive along in silence,
Dakota fields sliding by like dread,
like old traumas, a scream
plunging through night like a falling star.

The boy slows and lets her out
at a cross roads, corn on one side,
sorghum on the other. The night

is as hard to see through
as an angry face, a hand balling its fist.

A man says he has no spare bedroom.
She'll sleep in the barn, she says.
He nods, and calls his wife down, who makes
tea and puts a stale biscuit on a plate, with
a pat of butter. "Fresh out of jam," she says,
handing her the comfort she hasn't felt in years.

SURVEYS OF AN HOUR

The pale egg-shell sky cracks
here and there into blue,
the beyond of our eyes.

Something up there swims
in the region
of stars, while we stare
only to the frown
of impending rain.

I am no more visionary in a
landward direction than I am
at skyscapes.
The cracks in heaven widen
into jagged, sun-plated
canyons where no eagles fly.

This insufficient road
broken by wild oak
and pot holes, a shivering
black creek, implores us
to be mute, to empty our
minds of anxiety and regret.

Hold me, my wife says, and
I slip my arm over her shoulder
as the cold spreads out
across the hills.

A LITTLE KNOWLEDGE

What we know turns to dirt in our minds,
and if we are lucky, something might grow.

A little knowledge is like the rocks
in a parched field, each heavy with opaqueness.

When the rains come, the surface glistens,
the moist throat of the ground speaks

to the thunder, and hands reach up
out of darkness to invent.

A myth, as boneless as a worm,
will divide its tiny cell and tell a story.

A cold, hard inertia happy to be blind
will find a finger to dig with, and comes to.

More knowledge leaves the body panting,
afraid to move, to part the dumbness

we are born to, to heave more things
into the open, and stare at them.

Snow forgives us for our arrogance,
and the fog is a soft hand upon our envy.

Who will comfort us as we learn to speak,
and stand up ready to be dangerous?

THE ARC WE TRAVEL IN

At five, magic is the easy part.
All you need is a corner,
someone to sit close to you,
your small hand patting
the dark floor until an angel came.
Then you went through the wall
into the dusty, cob-webbed rafters
and followed a mote
of sunlight into heaven.

It didn't matter what happened next.
It was wasted already with
smells of dinner from below
and calls out the back door
for kids to come. Night was falling.
The long golden path we had entered
was a light in the hallway
and footsteps coming for us.

Now I sit alone,
the afternoon dripping over the sill
onto the rug, like slivers
from a squandered day dream.
The mice scurry in those secret
spaces I roamed, and hold
court where I had summoned the angels
with my incantations.

OUR COMMON LOSSES

The light settles into crevices
like pools of spilled water.
The neighborhood's black roofs
rise up jagged and mortal,
full of humans wondering
and of unforgiven blunders.

Waste not what is so rare
as the opening of a door, the light
pouring through and making
the weight, the inert immensity
float as if on floods of air.

These are my neighbors, and I watch
them pull down the shades,
rise to bedrooms like condemned prisoners.
They have no way to call,
their hands and mouths lie idle
as they go to sleep, gripped by fear.

Is no change possible, now that
we lie in the gutter of a world of death?
Covered in the blood of the fallen,
we hardly move our limbs but to shake
off the breath of vultures, the shadow
of killers we think are after us.

My town is dying; my street no longer
knit by common sense. The power lost

to gather up the pieces of a cup
that once held a common language.
Lies grow more tongues than our thoughts
could utter; ignorance is our only shelter.

WHAT THE DRUNK SINGS ABOUT

A drunk singing at the bar
searches his throat for a note,
a cradle rocking in his melted thoughts.
The ceiling light
hangs in a smokey heaven.

Ah, but in the ear that never heard before,
he sings like an angel.
Great hairy choirs belted
out the chorus, as he hoisted
a high note, highest of all,
a spear of grace cleaving the gloom.

The whiskey is a velvet stair
leading up to the clouds.
Down he reached
into a pocket where his soul rotted,
and found the linty trinket of a sound.

The marble mouth of God calls to him,
bidding his soul
to wake and follow him.
Under the great rose windows
he hears the heavens grind
away the morbid hours
before the daylight comes.

I WILL NOT PLEDGE ALLEGIANCE

Nationalism tastes like curdled milk
this morning. It sours the breakfast
waffles. The coffee stinks.
Patriotism is a pill I cannot swallow.
The tree is more important
than any flag pole, the flag soaked
in the world's blood. Let it fly away
like an injured bird, back to where
all symbols die when things go wrong.

But my memories make me love
some streets. Even the ones where
I grew up angry, or afraid, and fought
my way through recess and took
the hard shoulder on the way to class.
I loved the fall, the sycamores
peeling in the little park, where I
squirmed out of childhood
and put on jeans. The girl who looked
back at me stole my eyes, took
them home with her as I lay awake
blind with rapture.

My American days, each poured from a box
and soaked in ice-cold milk,
a candy bar to mark my afternoons.
Glazed doughnuts every Saturday,
before the piano lesson.

I am not brave. daring, angry
at foreigners. I do not believe in plots,
conspiracies, threats that have no name.
Fat Boy and Little Boy were
not my friends. I sat down in a corner
after Hiroshima and Nagasaki burned.
I could not feel a thing, but numbness
enlightened me. I was a lamb in a warrior
culture, and the guns would not be idle
for the rest of my days.

Gray battleships stood in the hazy sea
and came to port where we stared
up at them, all those riveted
plates of painted iron, the huge white
numbers stenciled below the bow,
the turret guns lowered and swaddled
in gray tarpaulins.
Young men in sailor blues
leaned over the cables to look down at me.
We said nothing; stared into each other's
eyes and turned away.

I pledge no allegiance, thanks
for not asking me to stand. I find
this rainy afternoon as good as any
in which to bare my soul, sitting down.

At the sweet spring, long long ago,
water trickled from a pipe in Pennypacker Park,
my father bent over with his jugs
to gather the fragile purity of America.

GOOD NIGHT, MR. AND MRS. AMERICA

The yard sale netted $117.52,
and the lawnmower was given away.
Funny how they pawed over
the stacks of dishes, wanted
everything for free. The sky
faded like a dream around them.

They bought on faith, or trust.
The tall boxes filled with foam
to nest a radio, a VCR,
his kid's computer
now soulless on the trestle table
in the yard. Nobody wants
old plastic, anyhow; it will go
to the dump this Saturday,
and the clothes, bending a branch
of a cedar tree, will be worn
on the backs of the homeless soon.

Mr. and Mrs. America hold hands.
Their troubles are around the next
corner, while they stand smiling
at strangers, taking coins.
He lost his job; hers hangs by a thread,
as if she were a spider building
a web in a dark corner.

She nukes the pot pies in the kitchen,
and shares the last beer. It's evening
in the middle of their lives,
without a car, a house for one more night.
No one to call or leave a message for.
Just the last warm sip of beer
before the evening sends them
up to bed, and lays them down
in a democracy that never weeps.

THE TYRANNY OF WEBSTER

Every truth grows a crust of deception
to protect it. It hides in a crease of mind
safe from logic, from any kind of reason.
It has no interest in time. It lacks
direction. It falls into the babble
of crib-dwellers and arises suddenly
in the gibberish of demented prisoners.

You find more gold in a stony hillside
than you will of wisdom. Gold
will mislead you every time. Wisdom
is worthless to a banker, or a pawnshop
owner whose bald head never
troubled over the meaning of existence.
Trust no one behind a counter.

The first time you lied to someone,
the mind retreated to a corner
behind your eyes. Your lips grew cold
when someone doubted the words
you depended on. A loose tongue
roams the desolation of the mouth,
not knowing where a curb begins
or a street stumbles into wilderness.

A LONELY WALK IN THE WOODS

The stream died right where I stand.
Black ribbon unspooled itself
in the soiled snow, and gave up
its ghostly will. A bird stands
over it, gazing down into death.

I admire the courage of the sky
to keep shining, to blister reality
with its glare, to hold the sun
in its palm as long as it can
before singeing its palms with fire.

I walk on, dragging my feet
over the scree of worn-down pebbles.
My closet is full of memories
hanging by a thin wire from a pole,
gorging on the dark around it.

THE PAINS OF GROWING UP

Someone bit me in the heart
and handed me the used apple.
I felt robbed of something,
my perfect skin, my protected core.

Teeth marks showed where
the robber had entered my
solemn privacy and tasted all
my secret emotions. I had to walk
home alone, the apple broken
in my pocket, the missing lump
of my integrity floating in the bottom
of a woman's gut. She was on a date,
laughing over her glass of wine,
enjoying the banter of a new lover.

I lay there in the cold glow
of night, observing how the stars
moved indifferently from me
to outer space. Their trail left
no luminous crumbs for me to follow.
I heard a knock on my door
and went down to answer it,
keeping a firm grip on the knob
to keep from falling in love again.

ALL THE FLOATING LIGHTS OF INFINITY

I hear my soul talking some times
as I sit here in glum silence.
I admire my hands, short-fingered
and wrinkled, "potato pickers,"
my father once said of his own hands.
Though he plied a razor skillfully
each morning and erased
the bristle from his round cheeks.
He admired his face, touched it gingerly
before skimming off the soap below
his puffy ears. I hear his voice even now,
clearing his throat, finding the proper
baritone note down in his bowels
to begin his greeting to me. Thank you,
I say, pulling on my school pants,
adjusting the belt, as he straightens
out my rumpled shirt and returns
to his delicate grooming. He was
a lady's man in his college days,
a regular wooer of the beauty
that floated through the narrow lanes
of campus, as each lifted her eyes
to observe him as he passed, tasting
the whiff of cologne he left behind.
He's old now, no, he's dead now.
But I am never without his breath
sweet with the last sip of a Manhattan,
and the feeling he had brought home

some wandering molecule of power
where he worked, in those long
grey corridors of the State Department.
Gone, but for a wisp of dust left
in my handshake before he died.

WHAT WE DO AT NIGHT

A poem pushes off the last of the snow
from its tenuous shoot. The wind is my friend
in the process, a breath from a hovering spirit.
Inspire me, I ask, bowed down like some
empty-headed student. I can't seem
to form a single word, I say. My teacher stands
over me, harsh and stern-faced, ready to send
me to the vice principal of rhyme. I pretend
to move my pen, but I am only scraping the paper.
What will form, I wonder, when the first darkening
of April wakes the dreaming earth?

Pushkin spoke in rhymed heroic couplets
over dinner, entertaining his guests
with startling images smelted out
of his molten eyes. And Byron wrote
off his cantos as if he were jotting down
idle thoughts to the darkness around him.
I whisper cautiously, crossing my t's,
breaking a stanza off and then welding
new lines to it, until a thought stirs.
The mill work of creation is noisy as hammers
stutter over the reluctant iron.
An anvil is there to break the back of silence
and pound out the next phrase.

One day my dead father will nod his head
in approval, even though he could not modernize
Lamartine into street talk. He wore an armor

of mechanical syllables, each one rusty
at the hinge, and ready for battle against
some dragon hiding in the trees. The virgin
cries out, the horse tenses for the rescue,
and the knight, slumped over his lance,
hears the plodding footsteps of authority
looking for him before he plunges his sword
into the heart of nothing to make music.

HOW THE WORLD ENDS

"It's coming, you can be sure,"
says one old farmer waiting
his turn in the chair. The barber
nods wisely, and goes on clipping
around a man's ears, as if he heard
something useful in his old age.

"It's all about the money," another
man says, pulling on his nose
as he reads a magazine.
He has the secret everyone is trying
to guess. He knows what's coming.
I pity him as he sits there, his money
evaporating out of the tall windows
of a bank and drifting out to China.

I take my turn at the chair
and immediately fall through the floor
into a realm of wonderment and magic.
The sun is setting over the rooftops,
the streets are empty. The rain
makes a mosaic of silver fragments
as the ordinary world disappears.

THE OSPREY

In honor of Sister Judy Tensing on Earth Day

The osprey, monogamous falcon
among nomads of the air, hatches
its young in hay and sticks
on tall poles, such as you find
along the highways in Vermont. I drive
the road three or four times a week,
going north among the grass fields
cultivated by dairy farmers
for their winter fodder. Great mounds of
hay lay buried under tarps, covered
in old tires to keep the wind away.

The osprey fledglings devour whatever
parents can snatch from rivers,
from reed-spiked swamps, the stagnant
lakes of rain-glutted fields.
Fish are said to go belly-up at the
sovereignty of nature, the crushing talons
of ospreys on the hunt. Icon of fidelity
in Chinese lore, voice of sorrow in Yeats,
loner among raptors preying on
glittering water sprites. Their cry is thin,
drawn across a silver wire in their throats,
a one-note violin played by a visionary
under the soaring galleons of summer.
Of all the taloned hunters of the sky,
I pray to you, glorious moralizer of my frailty.

Folded back wings, hanging hands in a dive,
you are powered to spy your prey
under cloudy water, and strike
in rapture, making your arc bend
like the light of the sun as it parts
the gloom and pulls the wriggling soul
of sacred life out of its hidden ways.
Who cannot love this world, when
the wings of such monarchs rise to rule
the unhappy ground and give us joy?

TWO

**... until whole utopias of intent
disintegrate into a waterfall.**

TEMPTATION

The candy store hangs open
to the street. No one comes along
to drool at its bins of candy.
The shadows are as thick as dullness
in a court room. You want to scatter
the fragments of despair left over
from growing up. But the old wooden
floor is worn out, and has no where
to go. The candy is a lure to the unwary.
It beckons potential sinners to the edge
to taste immortality. Sweet, cloying cylinders
of passion and indulgence await
the ones who have no souls to save.
The sun cuts up reality with a fiery sword.
All that is left of sobriety is my shadow
as I stand wasting away in ambiguity.

JOURNEYS ON FOOT

I'm partial to bogs, marshes,
sloughs, and heaths. Especially
Scottish heaths draped in gorse,
or wreathed in heather. Birds camp
in the thick of such flora,
tweeting softly to their lovers.

The bog festers with decaying life,
with soupy rivulets in the wake
of ghosts, and spasmodic rainbows
made by frogs entranced by ecstasy.
Nothing upsets the equilibrium
of these sweating Edens, until ice

grows a scab over their green estates.
Then a pawn shop opens its door
and offers dandelions to wayward
honey bees, and sedge stalks
to migrating geese heading south
where sunshine melts the hours into music.

AN ELUSIVE MOMENT

I follow the wind over the hill
to see where it sleeps at night.
It covers its silvery back
with sequins plucked from a galaxy.
Voices cling to its shivering arms
and slide away into the ooze
of discarded consciousness.

We're not friends, not yet anyway.
I haven't driven that far into
the unknown to meet it properly.
I know it has a name, a single syllable
carved from an oak burl, a nucleus
of thought no one had strung into words.

But a cap hangs in the sunset,
an envelope of emotion that never
found a mouth, or a heart,
but wound around a sliver of light
like silk blushing, like a smile
that almost said hello but not quite.

MY BEGGAR'S SOUL SALUTES YOU

Hello to the goddess of spring,
who sits primly in a low branch
overlooking my scrappy garden.
She has long legs, long hair,
her long fingers caress her skin
as she muses over a long memory.
She recalls all the flowers that ever were:
the rose blooms, the tulips swaying
like gondolas in the warm breeze,
the robin stretching over a nest
of blue eggs, each cracking open
as if a border were being broken
between the darkness of sleep
and the awakening to a noisy dawn.
She remembers it all, the attempts
to capture her rapture in the forest
as her sylphs and oreads danced
in celebration of new life. She looks
down at me as if I had come
to her modest chapel to ask a favor.
I only want to kneel and adore her.
Let the winds gather their fatherly
advice, the rain to dapple the ground
with inexpensive jewels, the hot light
pour out of heaven like molten crumbs
of gold from a smelter's oven.
Let the fine grains of evening sift
over her and drape her slender shoulders
in a silk cape covered with starshine.

I am grateful to see her here,
to know she will stay for the season
and let such mortal ears as mine
come to cleanse themselves
in the poetry of her every breath.

ON THE BANKS OF THE POTOMAC

The opal iris of the April sky
hangs within reach, as if
a rare and delicious liquor
pooled from the vein of a god.

We are off to the river
to catch some trout.
The cold, precise light haunts
the pockets of a rapids
like a girl's secrets, the kind
she only tells to best friends.

A trout hulas on my hook
as I pull him out; he lies there
in the creel turning stiff, with
the gold dust fading in its eyes.

Whatever grace this creature had
has been frittered away to foes,
alien creatures staring down
astonished at its solemn beauty.

FIRST CHORE OF THE DAY

The wrench broke in my hand.
I was hunched over a spigot
that had froze over winter.
The washer had dissolved
into pulp and water oozed
like the puss of a spider bite.

Cheap wrench, I guess. I saved
a dollar at a discount store.
I needed steel to overcome
the will of the snow, the ice scab,
the grip of death on the handle.

My father slapped me once
with his puffy hand; I had spoken
harshly to my mother, and he paid
me with a blow to my cheek.
He rarely hit me, and was loath
to hoist me onto his lap for a spank.

But he let winter overcome
reluctance when he made the hectic
sting my face. I didn't cry.
I looked at him the way a frozen
spigot looks up at me,
tingling from another's will.

Water lay meekly in the pipe,
wanting to flow, to soak its

lucid blood into the black earth.
It ached to embrace the dark
and clasp it to its heart
as spring arrived, and melted everything.

HOW NIGHT COMES ON

The land aches for a spirit, but even
the rivers have given up their church.

The moon saws at the far half of the sky.
I hear its panted breaths as it slips
behind the trees. Autumn has come
and we are without a feast day.

The wind has no name and moves
about the land like a widow, lifting
the straw to find her children.

Who will go with me in this golden
end of day, this seam in the night's
thoughts? I follow illusions that I love
more than the literal world.

The soul has a cleat on its shoe
to keep it from wearing out.
It rings like metal
as we tread the rocky wastes
beyond hope or faith.

WATCHING MACRON

He answers each hostile question
with a snarl; he is on TV, with
the collective face of France staring
at his every blink and tilt of head.
But the anger snakes from his pocket
and bites the microphone, as if public
were a kind of hex upon him,
and the government was a whore
sleeping with the masses.

The bankers are not satisfied.
They hover in the dark behind him,
demanding a new utopia – in which
the poor are devoured by taxes,
and the rich stand at the sluice gates
of their bank accounts.

A reporter's mouth says God damn
your betrayal of us, but Macron doesn't
read lips; he hears the whine
of pitiful self-defeat, the cry
of hopeless tradition dragging his feet.
There is a sun, he tells us with his
eyes, rising to blind us with its glory,
but you must follow him there,
not question where he takes us.
A blinding orb with Zeus' angry stare,
where mind is all, and flesh is the animal
tying us to dumb, unconscious nature.

His agile arms and bone-thin legs
are probed by a camera as he speaks.
He sits lightly upon his chair, folding
his arms on the radiant table before him.

What is there to fear? This is a debate, he
tells us, our mouths like old moons
with cusps drooping. We are on the path
to heaven, a gold-fenced road where
money and rationalism are the wheels
of our chariots, and a new Rome
is waiting to greet us when we come.

THREE TREES

Shaken by the storm, the leaves
are blown away. A final March wind.
The ground forlorn as
light trembles into dawn.

A worm is at work under
the stiff gray patches, gnawing
on obstacles in his progress,
until he feels a give.

Give is everywhere –
in wet branches, the bud ends
of briar bushes, the half-cracked
jackets of rose hips, the black stumps.

Silence is perforated with
the ticking of invisible birds,
their beaks raised to the turning air,
clearing their throats of fog.

A dusty sill, unwashed window panes.
A chimney grows cold
after the last freeze.
The house enclosed, entombed.

But light curls around a doorknob
and slithers through the crack.
A push liberates; each shift
unbuttons, and a shudder
disrobes the heart.

THE LATEST NEWS FROM THE BORDER

The wilderness creeps at night
into Minnesota, skirting the lake shore
while the nation sleeps.

In Wisconsin, sheets of rain
churn the Kickapoo River
into a flood of taffy-colored dreams.

The silt cradles its fossil bed
of didelphodon, Cuvieronius
glyptodon, and Goff's pocket gopher.

All blink, wear their muddy
Dior gowns, as they surge against
the wind, the flying houses.

Daniel Boone is nowhere to be found.
His rifle rusts over the mantle
of his cabin, now a popular museum.

Coonskin hat hung on a nail
in the nation's conscience,
while the shonisaurus snorts two jets

of steam into the morning air,
and the dire wolf points south,
each paw a note in the national anthem.

The bluffside cracks to let
a pygmy mammoth loose,
as giant beaver stir beneath the oaks.

The sulky earth lies spored with bones,
ghosts of blue gill, eelgrass limpets,
Lake Ontario kiyi, the shaggy dire wolf.

UNCLE JOHN

My uncle sat in a worn-out chair,
sunk down in the tired springs
where a thousand naps were conducted
after dinner. He would cross his legs
and allow me to examine his shiny shoes,
polished in the dim light of a bedroom
as he idled away his lonely hours.

He worked odd jobs around the pot-holed
streets of Brooklyn, unclogging sinks
with his battered tool bag of wrenches,
spare washers and plugs. He stunk
of caulk and the sour breath of wine.

He was often speechless at the mystery
of his life, amazed to have come this far
in his odyssey. He lit a candle
to his mother when he visited; the flame
wobbled on the dresser as he stared
into a dark corner, where she floated
out of reach of his nail-bitten hands.

He borrowed the air of worthier souls,
and exhaled his exhausted thoughts into the void.
Poor old Uncle John, no one ever loved you
enough to wake your spirit. You never
asked yourself a question beyond
the stack of dirty dishes in the sink,
the newspapers that burned brightly
with squandered dreams.

WHAT SCARS THE HEART FOR GOOD

for Joe Christensen, April 15 1941-May 28 1968

I held my brother in my arms.
He was as fragile as a primrose
as day thinned out into evening.

He was dying on the cancer ward
at a hospital of endless hallways
and voices talking in echoes.

The night was crumbling into flames
as the city mourned the death
of Matin Luther King. I saw

the nation's capital fade behind
the black smoke of the rage
and grief devouring what was left

of the American dream. Liberty
was drifting down the river
like a burning raft full of angry cries.

I am not bitter, I told myself.
But I lied. I drove through the acrid
streets clutching my brother's soul.

THE ANGUISHED HEART

The school bell rings
in the blind alley of my memory.
The sun is weakening
its anger in the sky, slowly
doddering into sunset.
Snow fell but not enough.
We are back at our desks
counting the minutes before
we are paroled.

My mother waits in the cold
yard, on the cement slabs
of a penitentiary.
She holds her purse against her
and looks up at the blind windows.
I am slumped over a copy book
scribbling my punishment
fifty times before I'm free to go.
Night spreads its soiled
wings over the roof tops.

On the kitchen table stands
a lonely glass of milk,
beside a leaning tower
of Oreos, a paper napkin.
My pilgrim soul has lost its way
and follows my mother's
footsteps through the dark.

THE CHORES

Inside each severed root
is a green vein gorged with
yearning, eager to
unwind the leaves of April.
But my pruners slice
the delicate wrist of each stem.

I am the law giver
holding back desire,
standing in the crumbling soil
of a garden, up to my ankles
in the grief of tenderness.

I am a stare in a crowded
room, longing for a woman's eyes
as she passes, her face asleep
in the bed of winter.
The heart is savage, a wolf
piercing the chaste bright air
with eager fangs.

GRATITUDE

The mountains keep crawling over
each other as I observe them
from the car. Bless them, I say,
as I pull into the supermarket parking lot.
Bless them all, their weary skins,
their weed-rough spines, their rabbit-
haunted corkscrew trails into
the briar thickets. Bless the bear
prints and their scat, turning gray
now that spring has unwrapped the buds.
Bless the clouds that drape their
ermine robes over them, and soothe
their loneliness. Bless the poor lunatic
who wanders with knapsack and
crooked walking stick, for he too
must lie down with the angels
when night covers his twisted wits
with sparkling stars. And bless
all those blue-black gleaming crows
who hunt the ghostly air of sunset
looking for a free meal. They too
whisper their needs to God and bed
down with spindly-legged comrades
as darkness drowns our human
souls in the waters of emptiness.

THE TORMENT

A flower unwinds
from a fist of ice. The earth
crumbles as the flower
loosens its grip, and begins
to turn a darker green.
Rain will melt winter's
palsied hand; a halo of silence
spreads over the hungry ground.

Someone is writing a letter
but leaves it unfinished.
The writer stumbles when
emotion becomes tangible.
It demands the truth, but words
are no help in this panic.
Better to leave the room,
and let the sun ravish
what you couldn't finish.

THE SECRET PRINCIPLE

The garden is leaving us.
It tugs at the earth to free itself.
It is moving north, following the wind
that carries weeds and wild flowers
ahead of it. Soon we will be left
with a tiny desert of gray soil
too sterile to generate more life.

Where are the birds this early morning?
I miss them already. Their song
is a tuning fork in my soul.
My watch has stopped, as if
my life were waiting for the next
beat of my heart. I live in suspense
of what will happen next.

THREE

We're all bound for strange fates.

THE GREEN MYSTIQUE

Oh to have money to burn!
The shops are all hungry
for my wallet; I can feel
soft lips aching to suck out
some twenties for a pen knife
I was admiring, tucked away
under a thick glass case next
to hunting knives, survival one-
blade daggers for killing a bear.
The fluffy green Astroturf they were
cradled in felt like a clearing
in a primal forest, one that called
to me like a siren as I stood there.
But no, those twenties had to go
a long way, and I didn't have
the courage to burn more lucre.
Not yet. But money, sweet cabbage
that had wintered in a forcing shed
of my checking account, was turning
a slight brown along the edges.
I saw a clerk smiling at her register,
gazing seductively at my expensive shoes.
She saw a plump goose standing there
responding to her attention, one that
would gladly get up on the carving board
and slide into a preheated over for a meal.
Ah, yes, even small fortunes attracted
the bees, the honey badgers, long-nosed
humming birds with wings beating twelve-

hundred times a minute. My poor wallet,
a fading beauty with worn bill fold,
an aging coin pouch, an overly-fingered
belly half empty now after my breakfast
with side of smoked salmon, and refills
of my coffee cup. One less twenty
to my citizenship, my right to cruise
the temptations of Main Street, the power
I possessed as firmly as a hand grips smoke.
It would break my heart to hand over
a wad of bills for a shirt I saw hanging
in the window; or a pair of shoes
on sale after the snow season.

ODE TO BETSY

My car rolls along on ancient bones.
The door creaks like a haunted house
when I get in. The mirror is always
gazing at the wrong side of the street.
I can't seem to yell loud enough
to get it to speed up when the light
turns green. We're getting older,
you and I, stiff in the shoulders,
wobbly in the knees, flabby when
the brake is pushed down on a turn.

I once heard Kenneth Burke say
that to get older is like borrowing
someone's car and not knowing
where the pedals were. He was
a spry old man, once the hero of rhetoricians
who read him with famished eyes.
Now he's just old, snow-capped,
gravel-voiced, careful with his food.
But he could get through three martinis
like a gambler and still be sober.

But my car, the muse of this poem,
still hauls me out of my privacy
into the world, thinking she might
be a pirate ship ready to loot a galleon.
But there's no gold piled up
in the holds of a ship long dead
and sunk in the depths of the Caribbean.

Clouds are gathering on the horizon
to deliver another rain storm, as my
engine stutters from the curb. The radio
lost one of its knobs, so the news
remains mute in the fuzzy speakers.
My air conditioner rolled over last summer,
a gurgle in its throat, a rattle in its lungs.
The junk yard leans over the fence
to admire its next cadaver as we pass by.

IN THE FACE OF AGING

Something gives and you are older.
The loose nerve swings in its space
like a disconnected wire. Memory's
hive of bees swarms out of the hole
and you are left guessing the name
of a certain face you still love.

Where was I then, you ask, standing
on the dry stones. Out there,
in the great openness of the weather,
the world lies in ruins. You are
alone, walking beyond the last outpost.
What will it take to find your
past again, strewn across the hills?

Or perhaps the past is drifting back
to its hidden world, and you should
let it. The silent floors of reality
are unlit, gathering dusk
into their unfeeling corners.
A chair projects its lingering brightness
into the evening, like a chime
on the failing breeze.

I am traveling without moving.
My bones unbraid their joints
from nests of cartilage.
I am longer in the arms, hands
reaching out into the remote

corners of a shell I inhabit,
feeling the cold, moist walls
that embody me.

My stars once held me in their arms,
danced with me at the shore,
in little clubs with a band
and a crooner washing the silence
with a drum and trumpet.
I held them in my heart as long
as I could, until they were as light
as the sparkles of the universe.

AT THE RAILWAY STATION

Things begin to blur, melt away
in the gloom of a living room.
A lamp floats across the dark,
as if carried by spirits away from the corner
where I sit. Nothing can make it
bring back the yellow light.

When I go out into the drizzle
and make my way through filthy streets,
I find the terminal soaring out of nothing.
Orphans gather at the entrance, eager
to beg for coins. They're hungry.
No one feeds them anymore

I gaze up into the vaulted ceiling, rusty
and inert as heaven, and just as empty.
A feeble thunder rolls away from the living.
The rain tries to reach the sea,
but the sea vanished from its stony bed.
A crowd moves slowly toward the trains.

We're all bound for strange fates.
No one has a ticket or a reserved seat,
just a small suitcase with nothing in it.
The children left school having learned
how to live without reason.

A cold air rushes to meet us as we stand
waiting to board. The tracks wander off
into the mist, disappearing into the unknown.

DRIVING TO ALTUS

After Oklahoma city, the iron-bleeding
earth breaks brick red under the plow,
a scab below the faded blue of spring.
A leveling of hills precedes the openness
as the road bears west; the sun
slants through the shot-gun window
until the chrome ignites like a welder's arc.

Thin, wiry fences drift over swells
like blackened moon beams. Out beyond,
thin spires and wisps of thread trace
the oblivion of distance
A bird hangs from the endless sky.

When the Plains open, the sky peels
away from the bony earth
like the flesh on a flensing knife.
Everywhere, the undulations
of mere matter simmer along the shards of ponds,
a clutch of weeds at the lip of every ditch.

Outward lay Lawton, and to the right,
through the harsh flatness, a town
called Altus – near Quartz Mountain.
Floating sideways among a false night
of trees, Ft. Sill spreads out its
squares of mown and suffering grass,
once an Indian school after the captivity
of 1874, now a shuttle of jets landing

and rising, each with a ribbon
of soot crumbling behind it.

A failed vision hovers over all;
the bunged fence guards nothing.
Even the cannon rusts in its toothless prayers.
A roof holds off the fury of the sun
but cannot lure a human dream, anywhere.

A PREMONITION

I had not thought to ask this photograph
what it meant before. It was a picture
of my mother leaning down to hold my brother
by his fingertips. Her hair had fallen
in her eyes, and her smile was vexed
by the intrusion of a camera.

The early '40s were cruel to her;
she had been lonely with my father away
at war, and the uncertainty of news
coming from the front. He could be dead,
he might be wounded in a hospital,
and here she stood in that strange light
troubled by the passing clouds, not knowing
if she were up to her tasks.

But there she was, steadying a boy
who would grow up and need her love
even when he moved away. He left a wound
in her heart that could not heal.
When he died, she lost her faith in god
she said, and sat for hours by his bed

Now the point emerges from her fingers,
holding up this fragile burden in her life;
the eyes obscure, the mouth not smiling
but turned under slightly, full of misgivings.
What was she thinking in that sunny fraction
of a day long ago, I wondered.

And why was she bending down as if
the earth were pulling cruelly at her
sleeves, her arms, her wobbly legs
in all that glory of late summer?

PONCA CITY, OKLAHOMA

Enid's embankment frames the main road,
and wheat fields swallow all ways leading out.
Grain elevators gleam like ice against blue heaven.
A ripple of sparks blinks
where the town keeps radio vigil.

It's harvest time, and combines
devour the sunny waves, leaving a wake
of dust and stubble. A grain truck idles
on a rim, lost against the drifts
Roll and heave, magnitude
without breadth of mountains.
We are flung forward in a spell of motor chants.

This is the mouth of autistic nature –
warnings rushing toward us with a word
or arrow between long gaps of silence.
Here and there, broken country watered
by wrinkled creeks. A town stirs
out of yellow sleep, gray spires in a stretch of nothing.
Ponca showing its flimsy face
against a steady southern wind. We are home
in the homelessness of the Plains.

A single gaudy mansion grounds the will
to earth, a man dreaming of greatness
when all he clung to was a scandal,
a girl-wife who danced like a feather
on his Italian balcony, over the T-shaped pool

and lakes he dug to mimic Tuscany.
That and a mismanaged fortune eaten whole
by J.P. Morgan, the crash of '29.
He moved to the servant's cottage,
sitting alone at sunset admiring his "big house,"
while the town impugned his Lydie
as a tramp and murderess,

The need to live grandly and feast
in the hunting hall on quail, wild turkey,
boar from his own fields under the pagan
frescoes of his ceiling, flouting
the dour Christian scowl of Ponca,
even as his money failed.

E.W entered Congress, became governor,
his Lydie hailed as "Princess of the Plains,"
their dream to conquer infinity almost
coming true, until their fortunes changed.
E.W. leaves the world heart first,
beaten by the odds, as Lydie turned hermitess
and fell in love with a meter man
who jilted her, left town with her last coins.

She landed in the slums of Manhattan,
came home toothless to live her final days
in the dim upstairs room where E.W.,
oil tycoon of a hundred million dollars once,
uncle, foster father, then husband,
died penniless. She too succumbed,
staring as the sun sank into the arid future.

One grass upon another, wheat or corn,
black grama once, each struggling upward
to the light, to drink the sky, then perish
against the iron will of time.
Each sunny row of days gnawed
by combines in an endless field.

GREEN TEA AND AFTERNOON

I am greeted by old friends
when I think back far enough.
The haze is like a cataract
and I barely make out shapes
that move in my past.
Or like the crumbling
of a photograph, creased
just where the eyes look
up at me with longing.

I cannot reach there with my hand.
I have no path to lead me
to the house, the afternoon
flowing over bricks
and down the hedge into
a dazzling sidewalk
floating somewhere in space.
The way is closed, and life
vanished from that corner.

But it is easy to slide from
one's eyes, to hold the thin air
of a memory in one's fingers,
raise it to the light
like a glass ball full of snowflakes.
Inside, in its own world,
are those friendships,
in a brine of forgetfulness.

AFTER THE FLOOD

River wrack strewn in the branches
of the willows. A muddy scar
stains the rocks, the pasture's edge.
A rage to devour has gone dry again,
with the river moping,
covered in gloomy shadows.

The parched tributaries are as
chalky as landfill, slabbed
and cracking in the July sun.

The land slumbers like a dog.
Time lacks grease to make things happen.
The wind coils round itself and
lifts the dust in an empty play yard.

A man looks out of a bedroom window
in his undershirt and scratches his belly.
He was almost drowned last year.
His house has the stale air of survival,
photos of the flood, the boats
snarling at the fierce current's foam.
The dresser is dusty where a mirror
cups the idle sunlight.

Fury washed away the ordinary world.
In the eerie light of a rainbow,
the sudden calm was like the grief
after a war has ended.

ONLY LOVE REMAINS

The figs I was saving for dinner,
luscious fat envelopes of sugar
and pale wine, have gone too soft.

The warm kitchen smothered them
with too much love; they gave in
like breathless school girls

to each soft caress, letting down
their guard, abandoning their mothers' wisdom.
Now they are mere knots

of pulp dying on a dish
in the pale light of a sick ward,
asleep almost, untouchable

to any mouth or lips.
The light had warned them
it would come, and now they sit

on the curb of oblivion, near
the rim of a garbage can,
under the hum of angry flies.

THE KISS

What do we hope for in a kiss?
The mouth is such a tiny spoon
for feeding us —

Cradled in each other's arms, we rock
back to infancy, the milk
sour on our tongues.

Here is my empty arm
I open like a door for you,
and you enter with dark looks.

I follow you down the stairs
into that low-hanging
consciousness where we strive

to make a life, pulling
illusions out of thin air
to make a shelter.

My tongue slithers in your purse
tallying your bank account,
your latest credit rating.

What will it buy you
but another flimsy claim
upon the exhausted earth?

Love slips away from us,
and we are left holding
its shadow in our selfish arms.

LUSTRUM

Every seven years the village *gardien*
goes up to the cemetery to clean house;
he scrapes the bones from the crypts
and tosses the fragile skulls to the ground.
Leg bones and hips fragile as tea cups
pile up with the still-intact fingers
of bleached hands. Time has gnawed
on each, licking the last mortal
shred of sinew from a knee cap, an ankle
poised to walk on its missing heel.

He sings in the crypt's dark air, sliding
the moody ghosts aside to take their leavings.
A fingernail hangs tenuously to its ledge
of flesh-eating stone before drifting
under his whisk. Nothing is spared
but the vanished breath, which dodges his
reach into the far corners. He casts
his fierce light into the crannies
of the other world, looking for teeth.
The dead are pliant and forgiving; they
keep nothing of their ties to this world.

He lies down on the cold unyielding bed
to rest. It is hot this July morning
with the blue sky drooped over its clouds.
The air is slivered into bird notes and
the erratic breath of the wind.
The living rattle their dishes in the houses

below, washing their hands, combing
the fine black hair back behind their ears,
smiling with all their nerves, their eyes
bright as opals in their living gaze.

THE SURPRISE

I had come into the room
suddenly, surprising her
with her shirt off.
She had her back to me,
and as she turned, her hands
cupped her breasts.
"These are only for the next ten years,"
she said, smiling." After that?

It was a cold pre-winter afternoon,
temperature around forty, with
the rain falling intermittently
past the windows.
Beyond, far beyond was the hazy
solemnity of the Adirondacks,
encased in mist, framed
by the awful silence of the trees.

We had been young all our lives.
Now we were old, talking about death.
It would never be the same, I thought,
as I left the room. We were strangers
in this familiar house, and I would
never know her as I did before.

IN ALL THE DARK RECESSES

A man sits by himself in a neglected park.
The pigeons are creeping around
on dirty feet looking for handouts.
His heart is bad; he has so little color in his face.
I dread his supper tonight — crackers
and a tin of sardines, a glass of water.

But he was a supervisor once, always
early at his desk, eager to begin the day.
His books were neatly arranged,
his checkbook balanced to the penny.
He shined his shoes, and ironed his own shirts.
No family to speak of, an old auntie
who died in a charity hospital, but who
wrote him elegant letters on his birthday
and helped raise him after his mother died.

But he retired early, thinking his savings
were enough. Someone gouged him on a roof
repair, and his note to the car company
was late one month. The repo man was
young and angry, and the car was gone.
His house sold for less than he needed,
and one by one the apartments he moved to
got smaller, and then the resident hotel
embraced him in its moldy arms.

THE END OF THE SEASON

I go down to the beach to watch
the American dream come to shore,
wave after wave of struggle,
hands dissolving into foam, teeth
grinding against the unforgiving sand.
A tide gives each stubborn surge
a friendly hand, and pushes gently
on the back to help it reach its goal.
But even the moon cannot descend
to earth without crumbling into
a trembling beam, a yellow-brick road
heading in the opposite direction.

A swimmer enters into the depths
of optimism. He's young, black hair
glistening as if he were primping
for his first date. But he is running
out of breath, gasping for air, feeling
a cold current wrap his legs
in an icy grip. He looks around,
wide eyed, gazing upon a shore
that trembles in the failing sunlight.
No one notices him. They are trying
to amuse themselves any way they can.

A bright red glare singes the end of day.
Someone left his floatie behind,
next to an empty pail, a bent shovel
that broke under the weight of doubt.

The wrapper from a candy bar is lifted
by the wind and given flight.
It rises above the sodden earth with
its salt grass and ghostly shells, a lost
utopia where children wander after
elusive visions, the summer promises
that once grew roses in their callused hands.

A MOMENT MADE OF WATER

A mourning dove sings outside
the window. Not even Shakespeare
possessed such syllables; it sings
from a hole in its emotions
deep as the Mindanao Trench,
where the worms are nearly invisible.

The names of once laughing faces
eroded from the heart. I loved
a woman once who could almost fly
in her slender bones. She floated
over gravity as if Newton had never lived.

A store sells old records out of dusty bins.
No one sings along when he plays one,
just stares off into space remembering
a vanished moment in youth.
My old jacket might still fit me, if only
I knew where I discarded it.

A man takes a cab across town. He has
a date, and is holding a rose in his hand.
He thinks she will still be there, waiting
for him long after the marriage ended.
I feel a pain growing in my breath,
and wish I knew how to comfort him.

THE GIFTS OF NATURE

Spring is thawing out my aspirations.
One by one, the ice melts a tear drop
of resignation, and I am young again.
I pull open the drawer and pick out
a failed effort I abandoned years ago.
It feels good to touch these words,
this elaborate maze of dead ends.
I know all my bad habits, and smile
at them. I am happy to be a failure.
It fits me like a hat, and the mirror
is my companion in this revelation.

The hill outside has moved closer
to the bedroom window. It wants
me to try again, even though last time
I staggered home with angina.
My knees feel like a walk, so I
take my imaginary dog with me
and we scale the modest rise
of ground as if it were Mt. McKinley.
I hear the birds as they drift back
from their sojourn in the south.

How kind the earth is, giving
a little, sagging where I come down
on my toes. Below is a kingdom
of waking insects, each stretching
new wings, sniffing for food, hearing
the thud of my footsteps on the roof.

A blur of sky darkens with the first
rain drops. I straddle the crest of rock
and stand there, covered in silver strings
like a mummer on New Year's day,
strutting in a home-made suit of glitter.

THE ROSES OF EDEN

I move among stifled spirits,
each running away from detection.
The world grows stranger
as I age, with the roses no longer
blooming in the dead of winter,
but alive and dew-encrusted
behind the freckled cheeks
of girls waiting for the school bus.

The prison down the road
collects the snow on its razor wire.
The doors of purgatory fly open
each time a bus arrives, and men
descend into the gloom of their sentences.
They are as empty as I am,
with the long corridors lit by suspicion,
and polished by hatred.

Snow falls in the higher terrain,
above the roofs of ordinary life.
It buries memory, and gleams
in the moonlight when everyone
tries to dream of childhood
among the roses of Eden.